Guiding Questions:

Productive conversations and planning for instructional coaches, administrators, and teachers

By Kristen Henry

Copyright @ 2019 Kristen Henry

All rights reserved.

ISBN: 9781095481851
Visit KHLiteracyEducation.com

Table of Contents

Introduction	3
Chapter 1: The Basics	7
Chapter 2: What is my learning outcome?	21
Chapter 3: How will I know if my students students are successful?	36
Chapter 4: Is my instruction aligned?	46
Chapter 5: How will I support all students?	53
Chapter 6: How will I collect data to drive my instruction?	61
Chapter 7: Scenarios	72
Chapter 8: Where to use the questions	82
Chapter 9: Questions in action	88
Chapter 10: Next steps	95

Introduction

Who knew questions could be so important? That question seems silly. Of course, they're important. We want our students to have active discussions, and we know that planning and then asking great questions helps facilitate that. But I'm not talking about questions that teachers use in the classroom; I'm talking about questions that teachers ask themselves, and questions that instructional coaches and administrators ask teachers. I'm talking about questions used for planning and reflection. These questions are pivotal. I didn't used to think that, but it has become clear over my years in education that a correctly placed question can make all the difference. It can guide thinking, it can offer guidance without a directive, and it can cultivate ownership.

But what questions should you ask yourself? Your teachers? Not all questions are created equal. Not all questions are right for the situation. The right question can illuminate and inform, lead to a discussion, lead to a revelation.

I was doing a presentation for a regional conference, focusing on highly-effective instructional elements in English Language Arts classrooms. As part of that I used two classroom scenarios with follow-up questions. To me, this was just a small part of the presentation, with a focus on what I was looking for in the classrooms. To the workshop participants, it became all about the questions. People emailed me after to get the questions. I had not intended for that to be the focus, but that's what it became. And at that point, I realized that in these questions people saw the power to better coach their teachers. I realized these questions were so important and could reveal so much, not only to the instructional coach or administrator, but to the teachers themselves.

Based on that feedback, I decided to write this, to offer insight into the questions that have worked for me, and how they can be used to drive your instructional coaching in a direction that benefits students and their achievement.

I've also added notes for administrators regarding T-TESS goals and which questions might be best aligned if they are working with teachers with goals in that area. Hopefully, this will lead to more productive post-observation debriefs and better teacher reflection, and, ultimately, building teaching capacity.

Chapter 1: The Basics – what you want to see in an ELA classroom

As the district-level content expert, I wanted to make sure my campus administrators and I were on the same page, speaking the same language. My solution to that was doing instructional rounds on each of my campuses. I would meet with administrators before to discuss what they wanted to look for, then do shared observations, followed by a debrief where we discussed next steps, follow up professional development, etc. In the first few years I started doing instructional rounds with my campus administrators, my main goal was for us to get on the same page about what made an ideal English language arts classroom. Many administrators don't have a background in ELA. In fact, for me, many of the administrators came from the athletic coaching world, so I made it my goal as the content expert to help them understand what I meant when I said quality ELA instruction. I shared what I thought were the most important things I wanted to see. But before we got to debriefing the lesson we just saw, it was important to create a baseline, a common language, a common vision. Then we could discuss what we saw from our own perspectives.

First things first - I am most interested in what the students are doing. The teacher at this point is secondary. For example, if the teacher is giving notes, I'm looking at her students. Are they attentive? Engaged? Bored? Off task? The point is, the teacher may be giving a fantastic and information-filled lecture, but if the students are disengaged none of that matters. It's not a successful lesson. At the same time, if I walk in and see a teacher off working one-on-one with student, I'm still looking at the students. Again, are they engaged? On task? Discussing? Or is the behavior off the mark? It's about what the students are doing. The teacher could be at the door dealing with a student worker with a message, but if the class is engaged and working, that's good stuff.

I want to see students reading, writing, and discussing every day. That's my bottom line. Are the kids actively engaged in reading? Or is the teacher reading a whole class novel to them for most of the period? Are the students engaged in meaningful writing or rote worksheets? The interconnectedness of literacy is echoed in the new standards for ELA in Texas, the TEKS. Every strand focuses on making sure students are reading, writing, speaking, and listening – which is what should be happening every day in an ELA classroom.

I want to see authentic learning (again, this is a component of the new ELAR TEKS) where the students see the relevance. I want to see instructional elements that are highly effective and proven by research. I'm a big fan of the Visible Learning research. In fact, all my teachers are expected to read and understand the text *Visible Learning for Literacy* by Fisher, Frey, and Hattie (2016).

My preferred framework is reader-writer workshop because it helps make sure that reading, writing, discussing is happening. It screams for mentor texts and peer work. It begs for engagement and authenticity. For my district, I use the following framework to help guide teachers.

Reading-Writing Workshop Framework

These are the required elements for each classroom and examples of how to implement

Reader-Writer Notebook

Vocabulary	Journal
Learning log	Reflections
Freewrites	Dialectical notebook
Interactive notebook	

Self-selected/Independent Reading

Free choice	Book talks
Literature circles	Silent sustained reading

Mentor Texts

Genre study	Genre definition
Close reading	Model texts for writing
In context grammar	

Mini-lessons

Direct instruction	Guided practice
Interactive notes	Modeling

Using both whole group and self-selected reading

Collaboration

Partner work	Group work
Collaborative writing	Peer review

Class discussion (both group and whole class)

Conferring

One-on-one	Teacher with small group
Student peer review	Author's chair

Through the rounds and the discussions and professional development that follows, I hope my administrators gain greater insight into what works for students to learn. And when I say learn, I mean learning for life, not just what you do to pass a standardized test.

A Few Definitions

Teacher clarity

When I write about teacher clarity I'm talking about how well the teacher understands what s/he is teaching and how that is communicated to the students. But it goes beyond just a well-written learning intention. According to Fendick (1990), there are four dimensions to teacher clarity: 1) clarity of organization, 2) clarity of explanation, 3) clarity of examples and guided practice, and 4) clarity of assessment of student learning.

Essentially a teacher must:
- Develop clear learning intentions
- Understand how to link all tasks, assignments, and activities to that learning intention
- Deliver the lesson in a way that is understandable and relevant
- Use examples that illustrate and illuminate the concept to the students, so they can eventually do the work independently

- Understand how to use assessment and feedback regularly to drive student learning

So just because the teacher has a clear learning intention, does not mean that they automatically have teacher clarity down, but it's the first and clearest sign that a teacher is clear about what they need to do for their lesson.

Instructional planning

When I write about instructional planning, I am talking about what should be happening prior to the lesson plan. Its focus is on the learning and how the teacher will know what the student learned. It is essentially focused on answering these four questions (or some version of them):

- What do my students need to know/learn/understand?
- How will I know that they learned it?
- What will I do if they struggle to learn it?
- What will I do if they already know it?

Teachers should, ideally, be able to answer these questions on a daily basis for their lesson. They are the foundation of a well-planned and prepared for lesson. So if you ask a teacher for a lesson outcome and they don't know it, or they don't know what type of assessment they're going to use, chances are they didn't adequately instructionally plan.

Bottom line

Students need to be reading, writing, and discussing authentic texts and issues every day in an English Language Arts classroom. It's about the students and where they are and who they are. It's about relevance. It's about instruction that is responsive to their needs.

So how do we all get there? It is surely not with hard criticism or mandates. It's through reflection, and goal setting, and asking the right questions of ourselves and others. It's about being thoughtful and not just doing what we did in the past. It's about all those things. But for today, let's start with the questions.

Part I: The Questions

These questions come from my experience working with and guiding teachers. To me, they help illuminate what is actually going on in a classroom – getting beyond what I may have been able to see. They also inform me where teachers might need additional knowledge and education. They may be unaware of a practice. In this way, the questions can lead to teachable moments. They also offer an opportunity for a teacher to ask a question. Maybe they have a question about how best to formatively assess. That question offers them the perfect opportunity to seek guidance where they may not have before. I've included five questions – but you might not get to all of them and you may need plenty of follow-ups. You'll also likely need to add a first question to get the conversation rolling. I usually start with "How do you think the lesson went?" or "How do you feel about the lesson?" Based on the answer to that first broad, open-ended question, I choose one of the five. I may start with number one and work my way through. It can lead to a very successful post-observation conversation, with reflection, learning, and goal setting. I invite you to try them, experiment, and make them work to your advantage. Make them your own. These are the just the jumping off point to quality conversations, planning, and even teacher collaboration.

The Questions

1. What is my learning outcome? What was your learning outcome? What did you want your students to learn today?

2. How will I/you know if my/your students were successful? Were my students successful? How do I know? What will I do?

3. Is my instruction and assessment aligned to the standards? Was your lesson aligned to the content and rigor of the standard?

4. How will I support all students (struggling, fast learners)? How did I ensure support for all students? How did you organize your groups/differentiate? Why?

5. How will I collect data to drive my instruction? How will you use what you learned about your students to move forward?

Chapter 2: What is my learning outcome? What was your learning outcome? What did you want the students to learn today?

I can still remember asking a new teacher what her learning outcome was for the lesson I had just observed. Her eyes widened like she was a deer in the headlights, and I knew at that moment where I needed to start working. It was clear that during the lesson design, warm-up and activity, the teacher had not taken a moment to actually define what the students needed to learn that day. Sadly, this was not the only time this has happened in a post-observation conference. Yes, this is probably the most important thing to know before designing a lesson.

Teacher

So how do you avoid this pitfall? I would suggest answering the question "What is my learning outcome?" It is the easiest and clearest way to define your work for the day.

Defining your learning outcome

First things first: define your standard. What standard or standards do you expect your students to master in this unit? Where will they start? How will you order the learning for maximum effect? Narrow those standards down to what you will focus on first.

But your learning outcome is not the standard. When I've asked the question "What was your learning outcome?" many teachers point to the standard on the pre-printed strip taped to the board. Most standards are deep and complex and aren't going to be mastered in one day. When I say learning outcome, I mean what the students are expected to learn that specific day.

For example, here is a standard from the new ELAR TEKS for 8th grade:

7(A) Analyze how themes are developed through the interactions of characters and events

Most likely, students are not going to master that standard in one day. How can you break up that learning? What from that standard can you expect them to learn in one day?

It might be broken down like this:
- Students will identify key characters in a short story
- Student will identify key events in a short story
- Students will explain the significance of characters in a short story
- Students will explain the significance of events in a short story
- Students will determine the theme of a short story

- Students will analyze how the author used the interaction of characters and events to develop theme
- Students will use text-evidence to support their conclusions

Notice these outcomes, taken individually or in a small cluster, are clear to both student and teacher. They are achievable in a day or two depending on your students and your timeframes. They are assessable.

In contrast, look at the goal below:
Students will read and analyze for theme

This objective could mean different things to different people and will likely leave students with little guidance. What exactly are they supposed to do? Most 8th graders won't get a clear picture from what they are supposed do during a lesson based on that objective.

If you cannot articulate the learning outcome for the day, chances are the students can't either. Teacher clarity is a key foundational piece to teaching (Fisher, Frey, & Hattie, 2016). Without it, many of the other perhaps fantastic elements that are going on in your classroom are less impactful.

Practice:

Take a look at the standards you plan to teach this coming week. Break them down into their elements and define what you want your students to learn every day. What can students tackle in a day? What can you assess in a day?

Teacher reflection:

But what if you haven't been using this question as a way to guide your instruction? Does it mean you haven't been producing focused lessons? Not necessarily. It can be helpful to also use this question, converted to the past tense, to reflect on your previous lessons. What was my lesson outcome? Can you articulate it? Was it clear to you and the students? Take a moment to think back on your last week of lessons. Jot down any revelations you might have about your lesson design practices.

Bonus points

If you really want to ensure students know what they need to do in class that day, go beyond the learning intention. Create success criteria.

As an example, let's pick one of the breakouts from the learning intention above.

Let's go with:
- Students will explain the significance of events in a short story

Potential success criteria:

- Students accurately identify three significant events in the short story
- Students accurately explain what makes the events significant
- Student accurately use text evidence to support their explanation

Administrator/coach

Asking the question "what was your learning outcome for the day?" gives the teacher the opportunity to reflect on their lesson in some depth. If they answer with little hesitation with a clear learning outcome or refer to a clear learning outcome posted on the board, it is clear the teacher has planned those out during the lesson design process. Now it's time for you to think through what you saw in the observation. Does what you saw match with the learning outcome the teacher has articulated. If not, it's time for some thoughtful follow-up questions. You might ask "Explain how today's lesson helped students achieve that outcome." Or maybe "Explain to me how you planned the experiences today to align to that outcome." If the lesson is not aligned to the learning outcome, these should help start the conversation that will lead to that awareness. It's important to listen to the answers. It might be that something that at once did not look aligned, is aligned when the teacher explains the larger context of the lesson.

This line of questioning can you help identify the following needs:
Teacher clarity – This gives insight into how well the teacher understands what he/she is teaching. Are the objectives clear? Is the planning clear?
Instructional planning – The quality of the answer to this question helps you see if the teacher has taken the time to do instructional planning. This is the first and most important question of that process.
Lesson planning – The answer to this question gives insight into how the teacher lesson

planned. Did they start with the outcome or the activity?

Content knowledge and expertise (T-TESS) – This gives insight into the teacher's content knowledge, shows how the lesson is linked to the understanding of objectives, including those from other disciplines. This also shows the opportunities or different types of thinking in the classroom, along with insights into the sequences of lessons and how they tie to the real world.

Achieving Expectations (T-TESS) – This question will help illuminate expectations and mastery of the objective. It gives insight into goals and whether or not the lesson is designed for all students to be successful.

> **Standards and alignment (T-TESS)** - This gives insight into the rigor and relevance of the lesson, as well as the integration of concepts, appropriate goals for diverse learners, and lesson design.
>
> **Knowledge of students (T-TESS)** – This can give insight into how the teacher is connecting the learning to prior knowledge of the students.

Now if I have the opportunity to talk to students while I am doing an observation, the first thing I will ask them is "what are you learning?" I don't ask "what are you doing?" I do this 1) because I want to re-emphasize learning in the classroom and not just the task at hand, but also 2) I want to see if students know and understand what they are learning – i.e. is the learning intention clear. For example, I was doing observations all on the same grade-level on the same campus. In one classroom – a veteran teacher's room – I asked a few students "what are you learning?" Even the silly boy in the back could articulate that they were learning to identify main ideas in a text so that they could later compare it to the film. The students in the class right next door, with clearly the same lesson plan, could not articulate the learning in the same way. Some gave me blank stares or tried to just broadly say that they were doing. These students also didn't seem to understand exactly where they were going with the lesson they were doing, while in the first class, students were engaged, on-task and moving at a nice pace. The teacher's clarity made all the difference in how the students tackled their learning that day.

Bottom line:

A clear lesson outcome is imperative to effective teaching and student success. Ensuring that both you and your students are clear on the desired outcomes helps everyone see where the lesson is going and how it's connected to the learning beyond that day.

Chapter 3: How will you know if your students are successful? Were my students successful? How do I know? What will I do?

In today's data driven schools, the focus is becoming more and more on periodic common assessments. To be clear, those are useful assessments that help teachers collaborate and share stories of success. What is this teacher doing in her classroom that makes her students so successful on that standard? That can lead to sharing of best practices and beyond. But what is also happening is the focus on these assessments and only these assessments to the detriment of the daily formative assessment that should be driving instruction, including differentiation and intervention. It's unfortunate when we wait for three to six weeks to really see how our students are doing. And that's where the second question comes in - "How will I know if my students are successful?"

This speaks directly to formative assessment and the definition of success for that day's lesson. So, you know your learning outcome. That's great. But how will you know if they got it?

Teacher

This second question asks you to define your assessment for the day. I would define this before creating any of your learning experiences or activities. I look at it like this, using the same learning intention from above:

Step one: Learning intention: Students will explain the significance of events in a short story

Step three: the actual lesson

Teacher model:
- Identify event
- Explain why it's important
- Give examples of text evidence that support explanation

Check for understanding
- List three events on the board
- Which is most significant? Why?

Guided practice
- Students are given an event in the story and must explain why it's important and provide text evidence

Independent learning
- Students work on formative assessment assignment

Step two: formative assessment

By the end of the period, the student will:
- Accurately identify three significant events in the short story
- Accurately explain what makes the events significant
- Accurately use text evidence to support their explanation

You essentially define the outcome, choose the assessment, and then go back and fill in the lesson.

Examples of formative assessments:

- Exit tickets
- Observations
- Writing assignments
- Short answer response
- Group/partner work responses
- Teacher-student conference

It's not enough to just come up with an assessment, though. You must also define what success looks like on that assessment. That's part of your planning, too. You should be able to look at those exit tickets and know where your students are. And then use it. This assessment directly informs what you will be doing in class tomorrow. Is the entire class lost, necessitating a whole group targeted lesson? Or is it just a handful of students that you will need to either pull for small group or conference with individually? Here you can see the power of daily formative assessment. You can intervene immediately instead of waiting weeks for gaps to grow wider, becoming harder and harder fill in tier 1 instruction.

Reflection

Now take a moment to reflect on your past week of instruction. What formative assessment did you use? Did you use it to drive your instruction? How? If not, why aren't you? What can you do to improve your use of daily formative assessment?

Administrator/coach

Daily formative assessment is what drives instruction. This is the most effective way to respond to the needs of the students and intervene early, before gaps can grow larger. The follow up question "How do you know if your students were successful?" gives the teacher the opportunity to articulate her formative assessment process for that day since it may have been something you didn't explicitly witness. An exit ticket is pretty easy to see, but teacher observation might be more difficult.

There is also the opportunity to ask follow-up questions: What did success look like today? How will this drive your instruction tomorrow? The rest of the week? What will you do in tomorrow's lesson based on what you learned today? These are all jumping off points to conversations about the use of formative assessment on a daily basis and how the teacher uses it.

This can help you identify the following needs:
Teacher clarity – This gives you insight into how clear the teacher is in his/her or understanding of the assessment and how it aligns to the rest of the lesson.
Formative assessment – This shows the teacher's understanding of the use and timing of formative assessment.
Monitor and adjust (T-TESS) – This can illuminate how a teacher gathers input, gives academic feedback, and checks for understanding.
Data and Assessment (T-TESS) – This shows the teacher's understanding of both formal and informal assessments, student self-assessment, feedback, and progress monitoring.

Bottom line

Teachers need to know where students are in their path to mastery on a daily basis. It allows just-in-time intervention and responsive instruction. If educators wait weeks for a common assessment, valuable time and opportunity are lost. Daily formative assessment ensures teachers have the pulse of their classroom and can plan the best lessons possible to reach students.

Chapter 4: Is my instruction and assessment aligned to the standards? Was your lesson aligned to the content and rigor of the standard?

I have walked classrooms with campus administrators many times in my career, completing instructional rounds to get a clearer view of the state of a certain department. It is not uncommon to walk into a classroom and experience an engaging lesson. The teacher is clear, the students are into it. The administrators are happy with what they see. And I get to be the naysayer because I'm the one who better understands the standards and how they align vertically from kindergarten through high school. Yes, that was a great lesson – if this were a fourth grade class and not a seventh grade class. It's a deflating conversation for everyone, but the fact is there was good stuff going on in the classroom. But if seventh graders are supposed to be evaluating works of nonfiction instead of just identifying text features, we've missed the boat.

So how do we ensure alignment every day when we walk in the classroom? We have to take the time to ask the question: Is my instruction and assessment aligned to the standards?

This takes all the steps we've done before to get accomplished. We have to look at the standard, our breakdown of learning outcomes, and our definitions of success. If we are on the final day, with the final learning outcome, and the standard says evaluation, but our students are still at the identification stage, something is amiss. Did our assessment not give us reliable data? Did we effectively use our assessment? Are we just doing a stock lesson because it worked without looking at the bigger picture?

These questions ask us to critically look at our lesson design and pedagogy. We have to be honest with ourselves about whether or not what we are doing is getting our students where we need them to be at that grade level in that subject. After all, we have been assigned to teach a particular grade level. This guided question can help us do that.

While reflecting on alignment questions, it might be useful to use a vertical alignment document if that is available. What is taught at the grade I teach? What about the previous year? What about the year after? This can help you differentiate what you are responsible for this year.

Reflection:

Think about your lessons last week. Look at your learning outcome, your standard, your assessment. Do they align? Does your assessment speak to that standard and if your students have mastered it? Was your instruction aligned and therefore a good preparation for the students to be successful on the assessment?

Administrator/coach:

Many times teachers get excited about a new activity or their favorite activity of the past. Teachers are busy and having something already in the bank saves time and energy. And certain activities are just plain fun. But do they get the job done? Do they lead students to mastery of a particular standard? Are they moving instruction forward? When you look at the year, teachers often have fleeting moments with their students. Every minute matters. So it's important that when the students are in the classroom and primed to learn, they are learning what they need to for that grade level.

Asking alignment questions guides teachers to reflect on their alignment and how important it is. Are those experiences really going to help your students master that content?

This will help you identify the following needs:
Teacher clarity – This gives you insight into how the teacher understands how the standards are linked to the lesson – activities, assessment, etc.
Standards & Alignment (T-TESS) – This gives insight into whether or not the lesson is aligned to the TEKS, if it logically sequenced and connected to the broader unit. It also gives insight into the teacher's lesson design process.

Bottom line:

We have a finite amount of time with our students. Often times, we have even less time before a high-stakes state assessment. Basically, we have little time to waste. If we want our students to master the rigor of our standards and be ready for the next grade-level or challenge they will face, we have to teach at that level as soon as we can. It may be tempting to stay on an activity that is fun and engaging but at a lower level, but it's our job to get them to reach higher and be ready. That means figuring out ways to make that higher level of difficulty or complexity also fun and engaging.

Chapter 5: How will I support all students (struggling, fast learners)? How did I ensure support for all students? How did you organize your groups/differentiate? Why?

I love the concept of PLCs. I've enjoyed being a part of them. One drawback, though, becomes this false idea that if everyone plans together and has the same lesson plan, that all their classroom instruction should all look the same. Here's the problem: you can't successfully differentiate and every classroom look the same. Each classroom is made up of different students with different needs. Assessment will drive instruction in different ways. If one teacher's class understands one concept, but the other teacher's class doesn't, the latter will need a whole group focus lesson. The first one won't. He may instead need a small group to reinforce the concept with the few students who are struggling. That is not going to look the same.

That doesn't mean you can't use PLC to better differentiate and bring in best practice. PLCs can be used to help anticipate where students will need differentiation. How could I potentially help my students that struggle? And what am I going to do with those students who get it in the first 30 seconds?

Teacher

It's important to know beforehand how you will differentiate in your classroom. It's part of quality instructional planning. How are you going to support all students?

This planning takes anticipation and experience. It may also take collaboration with your itinerant support teacher or your gifted and talented specialist. But if you can answer these questions before your lesson even starts, chances are you are set up for success.

Reflection

Think about the past week. What did you have in place to ensure all students were supported? How did you use that plan? If you didn't have a plan, how did that work? How can you better prepare to support all students?

Administrator/coach

Sure, differentiation can happen on the fly – sometimes. But the best way to differentiate is to be prepared. If you need text at a lower lexile level, you need to have that printed and ready to go. If you need more difficult sentence combinations for your super stars, those need to be ready to go, too.

Effective differentiation is planned ahead of time and implemented flexibly.

These questions help you get the teacher's deeper understanding of differentiation. Too often this is seen as something for tutoring or the RTI teacher, but differentiation is part of all effective tier 1 instruction.

This will help you identify the following needs:
Differentiation (T-TESS) – This can show how the teacher adapts lessons, monitors student participation, differentiates instruction, and prevents student confusion.
Instructional planning – This again speaks to whether or not the teacher has gone through the

instructional planning process. This speaks to questions three and four: What do I do if they struggle? What do I do if they already know it?
Date & Assessment (T-TESS) – This gives insight into the teacher's analysis of student data and how they are using formative assessment to make instructional decisions.
Knowledge of Students (T-TESS) – This gives insight into the teacher's knowledge of students' prior knowledge, adjustments made tied to student needs, and opportunities for students to utilize individual learning patterns.
Activities (T-TESS) – The answer can speak to goals, student ownership, using technology to actively engage student ownership, and how the

teacher may or may not have used grouping to help reach and support all students.

Achieving Expectations (T-TESS) – This will give insight into whether or not a teacher has students setting goals and is helping all students attain mastery.

Content Knowledge and expertise (T-TESS) – This can give insight into how well a teacher anticipates student misunderstandings.

Monitor and adjust (T-TESS) – This gives insight into how a teacher monitors and adjusts for student engagement.

Standards & Alignment (T-TESS) – This gives insight into whether or not the teacher has planned appropriately for diverse learners.

Bottom line

You need a plan to support all students. You know your students. You know the potential misunderstandings and you need to be proactive rather than reactive. You need to be prepared, so use these questions to help you be ready for whatever your students bring that day.

Chapter 6: How will I collect data to drive my instruction? How will you use what you learned about your students to move forward?

We know providing feedback to students is highly effective (Fisher, Frey, & Hattie, 2016), and that it drives their learning. But how does student work also drive our instruction? How do we use it to move forward? I've always responded to Fisher and Frey's (2011) concept of feed forward – using the evidence we've collected in the classroom to inform and develop our instruction. But that means teachers must collect evidence every day. As Rick Wormeli (2010) says "I should be able to walk down a hallway, stop a teacher cold, they don't know I'm coming, they don't know the question's coming, and say how did formative assessment inform one of your decisions today or this week ... and the teacher should feel very comfortable" answering this question. This question helps teachers plan and reflect on how they collect evidence and then use it to shape their future instruction.

Teacher

Every day is essentially a fact-finding mission. We teach; we collect data. We work with a small group; we collect data. We use many techniques to find the best data. We use frequent checks for understanding, student observation, both spoken and written student responses. The classroom is filled with data. But are we using it?

Ideally, during key points in the lesson and at the end of the period, teachers have collected data that does two things. It 1) lets them know where their students are at that point in time toward mastery of a certain goal, and 2) lets them know what needs to happen in that very lesson or the lessons immediately following. This allows the teacher to 1) intervene with students who need it in real time and 2) adjust the lesson if necessary to meet the needs of the class. If those things don't happen, students may be left confused, gaps may grow, and time is lost because teachers aren't making the necessary instructional moves to end the confusion and cut the gaps off at the pass.

So this question becomes an imperative one to ask every day.

First, what data are you collecting? Have you built in and planned checks for understanding within the lesson? Or you using an exit ticket or other form of formative assessment at the end of the class? This is tightly aligned to question 2 but takes it a step further. It's not just the how you will know if your students have learned, it's what have they learned, and what are you going to do about it?
Checking for understanding during the class may inform how you will pull small groups for guided

instruction. It may help you prioritize which student to conference with. An exit ticket at the end of class may help you create groups for the next day. Or it may help you figure out the appropriate mini-lesson. Either way, these are important decisions that allow teachers to effectively differentiate every day in tier 1.

Reflection

If you find that you haven't been collecting evidence or using the evidence you have collected, it's time to think about how you are going to start. How are you going to plan your lessons to include opportunities for you to collect evidence? Once you have that evidence, what are you going to do with it?

For example, if you check for understanding and discover a handful of students don't understand the concept, what will you do in response? Are you prepared for guided instruction? Conferring? Do you have a plan to take what you have learned from your formative assessment and use it to benefit students?

One way to do this is to build in guided instruction. You have anticipated that not all students will master that day's content. You proactively plan a check for understanding before students are set to work in pairs. You notice four students communicating that they really don't get it. Using that evidence, you pull the four to work with you in a small group. You give additional instruction and provide feedback. You used what you learned right in the middle of the lesson, just in time learning.

You may also use evidence to inform future lessons. During that same lesson, you end the class with an exit ticket. While your monitoring in the hall between classes, you review the exit tickets. You use the students' answers to help you sort them into groups. You notice three students are significantly behind in their understanding. You plan to work with them in a small group tomorrow. You group the others in heterogenous groups to work together on the next assignment. Again, you just used the evidence you collected to feed forward and benefit your next lesson.

Administrator/coach

Gathering evidence and using it for instructional purposes are key elements to quality differentiation. It's not enough for a teacher to assess their students. They need to use that information to drive their instruction. If you notice a teacher does gather evidence, you can ask: How are you going to use the evidence you gathered today? If they haven't been using formative assessment, you might ask: how do you plan to differentiate? What are you basing those decisions on? This will force teachers to reflect on the connection between assessment and instruction.

This will help identify needs for:
Differentiation (T-TESS) - Does the teacher monitor the quality of student participation? How?
Monitor and Adapt (T-TESS) – This gives insight into whether or not a teacher systematically gathers input and checks for understanding.
Data and Assessment (T-TESS) – This speaks to how the teachers uses both formal and informal assessment and analyzes that data.

Bottom line

We have to know where we are before we can build the roadmap for where we need to go. This is a constant daily activity that requires planning, observation, and deliberate evidence collection. Teachers can grow their own effectiveness by reflecting on their use of evidence in driving their instruction – not just during a benchmark, but on a daily basis during tier 1 instruction.

Part II Using the Questions:

You are armed with these five questions. Now what do you do with them? Remember, they are only a vehicle to assist you. You still have to know how to use them effectively. Part II focuses on putting these questions into action and looking at where you can use to your greatest benefit.

Chapter 7: Scenarios

Let's put it into practice and look at some scenarios you might see as you walk classrooms. As you read each scenario, think about how you would approach the post-observation conference.

Scenario #1:

The teacher is giving directions to the students who are sitting in groups of four.
On the board: Agenda: 1) Warm-up 2) Group work
The directions are clear, and the students get to work on a poster about a story they have already read. You ask the students what they are learning, and they respond that they are making a poster. You ask again "but what are you learning?" The

students just talk about the story they read and the directions.

Think about what questions you would focus on.

Spots for clarification

I think it is clear you need insight into what the learning outcome of the lesson actually was. It is not posted, nor can the students articulate what they are learning. Depending on the teacher's answer, the questions might stop there. If the teacher cannot articulate the learning outcome, that's where you need to start. Work needs to begin on instructional planning and ensuring the teacher has a clear idea of what they are teaching, otherwise the students will struggle to identify their own learning.

If the teacher can articulate the learning outcome, it becomes a slightly different discussion. How can she better explain the learning to the students? Would it help to post it on the board with success criteria? How could that help illuminate the learning for the students?

Scenario #2:

The students are working independently on reading analysis questions. On the board: Students will make inferences and support their understanding with text evidence.

Success criteria:

- Students will accurately respond to the questions
- Students will provide at least one example of text evidence to support their answer
- Students will provide at least one line of explanation that connects their evidence to their answer.

The students work until the end of the period when the teacher picks up their work.

Think about the key areas you would like to ask about.

Based on the board, the teacher will likely have a clear answer for the first question. The second question could though provide insight into how the teacher is going to use the answers. The success criteria show you she has at least defined what success looks like.

The question about alignment could give you some insight into where she is going with the lesson and how it ties into the bigger picture.

The question about supporting all students will be important for this discussion. There is not visible evidence that the students' work has been differentiated or that any extra help or extension was in the plan. The answer to this question could give you insight into how the teacher plans on helping all students be successful.

The last question will help you see how the teacher will use the student answers to build future lessons

Scenario #3:

Students are actively working in groups.
On the board:
Students will work together to comprehend text using the reciprocal teaching protocol
Success criteria:
- Student's notes will indicate their predictions, questions, and summaries from their table discussions

The teacher moves around the room to check on students but spends most of her time with one group.
Students turn in their notes (in the form of a foldable) at the end of the period.

Think about what you would focus on.

I would likely ask the question about supporting all students. I would want insight into how she formed her groups and if she purposely put students together, so she could provide added support to the group she stayed with the longest. Also, how did she feel the reciprocal teaching protocol helped all students?

I would also look at the last question. How is she going to use the student notes to inform her future instruction? Will this influence her future lessons? Future group composition?

Scenario #4:

Posted on the board: students will analyze figurative language in poetry
Students are working on a handout where they must identify the figurative language in a poem. The work is independent. The teacher circulates and helps individual students as needed.

Think about what questions you would focus on.

The question that sticks out to me would be dealing with alignment. The learning intention calls for analysis, but the assignment only calls for identification. That is clearly not aligned. You might ask if there will be follow up in the next lesson. Either way, the activity should match the learning intention. You could also get additional information from the rest of the questions that would help you determine how the teacher will use the handout as formative assessment or data and how the teacher supported all students.

Conclusion

Hopefully these scenarios gave you some insight into how you could focus on specific questions to drive your post-observation conference. There are some elements that become clear in an observation and there are some that don't. The questions can help you gain insight into what the teacher is thinking and where the lesson is going. Often times, this can help you better interpret what you saw. Other times, it will beg for more follow-up questions. Those questions are up to you, but at least the initial questions provide guidance. I hope these scenarios also help you think about some areas to look for that you might not have thought about.

Chapter 8: Where to use the questions

As noted earlier, there are different ways these questions can be used. They can help drive instruction, reflect on instruction, plan lessons, or debrief after an observation. In the end, they are all about gaining awareness of instruction and where it needs to go. They are the vehicle to quality conversations that end with positive impact on students and student success. Don't limit these questions to the post-observation conference. There is much more work they can do.

Planning

Teachers, if you can answer all these questions about a lesson, you probably have a solid lesson. Clear learning intention: check. Success criteria: check. Planned formative assessment: check. Differentiation: check. Evidence to feed forward into future lessons: check. That might seem simplified, but if you have that clear a vision of your lesson and your content, you understand what needs to be done. You know where you need to go. You aren't wasting time because you know where you need to get those kids.

It could look very differently. I've observed many a class where the instruction seems to be going nowhere. It just floats along. Journal here. Reading assignment there. Some juggled pieces tossed together. There's wasted time. The pacing leaves much to be desired. No one in that classroom, teacher included, knows where that lesson is going or how it's attached to the larger learning objectives. It's just… there. This is what happens when a teacher doesn't have a clear vision of what the students need to learn that day. Now, it might just be one of those days, but what if it's not? What if that is more often than not how each day goes? Students are missing out.

Think about the classroom you want. Is taking the time to answer five questions worth having a focused, clear lesson every day? I would say yes. Absolutely. Your students deserve it.

Post-observation Conference

I clearly developed these to help me with post-observation conferences. My first year in my position, I remember floundering to have quality conversations about doing walk-throughs. How could I get to the core of the issue without insulting the teacher or making them angry? That would have been counterproductive, damaging a new and tenuous relationship. My answer to that was reflective questioning. There's no gotcha. It's about bringing an issue to the teacher's attention in a way that helps them realize where they need to work or where they need more information. It's about giving them ownership of where they need to go. Will this always work? Of course not. It's not a silver bullet. It's just a vehicle to assist you as work to build capacity in your teachers.

Professional Learning Communities

The email came from a new campus instructional coach – "I need help. I feel like my PLCs are falling apart." I showed up to our already scheduled check-in meeting and we started chatting. She was struggling to find ways to help her teachers effectively plan. This was when I was beginning to put together this resource. I had my questions with me, so I pulled them out and said, "maybe these will help." I suggested she ask reflective questions as her teachers planned. She wouldn't be telling them what to do, but she would be guiding them along the way.

When I returned a few weeks later, she said the questions were helping her guide PLC. The questions aided in the planning for her teachers and helped her structure PLC.

Chapter 9: Questions in Action

But what do these questions look like in action. This chapter is made up of some of my real-life examples from working with teachers. The discussions are based on my notes and are not word for word. They have also been edited for clarity and length. My hope is they give you an idea of how these conversations can go and how they can be used.

Teacher one:
Me: How do you think the class went?
Teacher: It went well. I had them do their independent reading and then they worked on

their personal narratives. I think they've been working well.

M: So what was your learning outcome today?

T: They're working on their personal narratives. I want them to add figurative language to their writing. I gave them this (shows me handout) to help them.

M: So how will you know they are successful?

T: From their writing – I'll get their final drafts back and look for their examples of figurative language.

M: This is their performance assessment from the curriculum, right?

T: Yes

M: So it's aligned... ok

M: So how do you support all the students?

T: I do a lot of one-on-one, working with them to give them feedback.

M: How will you use what you see in their writing to move forward with your lessons?

T: It's really about going back to do more practice. I might have to go paragraph by paragraph to help them integrate figurative language. It's really about practicing writing. That's why I also do warm-ups about sentence structure – to help them with their writing.

This conversation reinforced what I had observed in this teacher's classroom and gave me additional information about her feedback process.

Teacher two:

M: How do you think the lesson went?

T: Well, they took a quiz and then they just had time to finish work they had missed.

M: So what was your learning outcome for the day?

T: Well it was a quiz, so how do I put that into a learning intention?

M: Well, you could put the students will demonstrate their knowledge of vocabulary. Your assessment could be defined in the success criteria.

T: Oh, ok.

M: What was the outcome of the other assignment they were working on?

T: They annotate an article every Monday. (Shows me directions for annotation and questions).

M: So do you evaluate the annotations?

T: Yes, I look to see if they are off or not. And so today, they had turned them in, but they were not really complete, so I wanted them to work on them some more. I didn't want to accept what they had done.

M: So they have an opportunity to re-do for mastery?

T: Yes.

This conversation offered a few opportunities. One, it allowed the teacher to ask about learning intentions and success criteria. This became a teachable moment. It also allowed her to explain what may have otherwise looked like a lackluster class. Instead of students just doing worksheets, it was students working toward mastery. That leaves me with a very different impression of that lesson and teacher than had we not had the conversation.

Teacher three:

M: So what was your learning outcome for today?

T: They're applying what they know about personal narratives and using the writing process to write their own narrative.

M: How do you know they are being successful?

T: I'm looking at their graphic organizer and their plot diagram.

M: So you're checking it to see if they are getting the concepts?

T: Yes.

M: So how do make sure all students get support?

T: Well, seating. I know she gets distracted, so I have her work by herself. Those two students work a little slower, and they work well together and help each other so I put them together. That one girl I also give additional notes.

M: So how will you use what you collect to plan your lessons?

T: Well…

Here were also have a teachable moment. The teacher is new and clearly doesn't really understand what I meant by the last question. This gave me the opportunity to explain how to feed forward and be responsive to student needs.

Chapter 10: Next Steps

Where to go from here? It's time to take these questions into the classroom. Get them into the action. But how do you start? First, make sure you know and understand the questions. Hopefully this resource has helped you do that. You can also use the observation template in the appendix to help you organize your thoughts. Finally, practice! Start using the questions and the more you use them, the easier it will be and the more it will make sense.

Happy questioning!

Appendix:

Instructional planning template

Reader-Writer Workshop Framework

The Questions

Observation Template

	M	T	W	T	F
What do my students need to know/understand?					
How will I know that they understand it?					
What will I do for those who don't understand it?					
What will I do for those who already know it?					

Reading-Writing Workshop Framework

These are the required elements for each classroom and examples of how to implement

Reader-Writer Notebook

Vocabulary
Learning log
Freewrites
Interactive notebook

Journal
Reflections
Dialectical notebook

Self-selected/Independent Reading

Free choice
Literature circles

Book talks
Silent sustained reading

Mentor Texts

Genre study
Close reading
In context grammar

Genre definition
Model texts for writing

Mini-lessons

Direct instruction
Interactive notes
Using both whole group and self-selected reading

Guided practice
Modeling

Collaboration

Partner work
Collaborative writing
Class discussion (both group and whole class)

Group work
Peer review

Conferring

One-on-one
Student peer review

Teacher with small group
Author's chair

The Questions

1. What is my learning outcome? What was your learning outcome?

2. How will I know if my students are successful? Were my students successful? How do I know? What will I do?

3. Is my instruction and assessment aligned to the standards? Was your lesson aligned to the content and rigor of the standard?

4. How will I support all students (struggling, fast learners)? How did I ensure support for all students? How did you organize your groups/differentiate? Why?

5. How will I collect data to drive my instruction? How will you use what you learned about your students to move forward?

Observation Template

Teacher:_____
Date:_____
Period: _____   Prep:_____

Learning intention:
- Visible, clear, and student friendly
- Student can articulate learning for the day
- Success criteria posted, clear and student friendly

Notes:

_____

_____

Formative assessment
- Teacher checks for understanding
- Formative assessment tied to success criteria
- Use of exit ticket, observation, checklist, writing to assess

Notes:

_____

_____

Alignment
- o Learning intention is aligned to context and rigor of standards
- o Experiences and activities are aligned to intention
- o Assessment is aligned to intention and success criteria

Notes:

_____

_____

Differentiation
- o Scaffolds are imbedded and pre-planned
- o Students are able to:
  - o Work together
  - o Choose texts
  - o Choose assignment
- o Group work is thoughtfully planned

Notes:

_____

_____

Use of evidence
- o Teacher collects evidence throughout lesson
- o Teacher responds appropriately to evidence collected – i.e. check for understanding, etc.

- Lesson is driven by previously collected evidence

Notes:

_____

_____

Comments for follow up:

References

19 TAC Chapter 110. Texas Essential Knowledge and Skills for English Language Arts and Reading from http://ritter.tea.state.tx.us/rules/tac/chapter110/index.html. Retrieved April 26, 2019.

Fendick, F. (1990). *The correlation between teacher clarity of communication and student achievement gain: A meta-analysis.* Unpublished doctoral dissertation, University of Florida, Gainesville.

Fisher, D. & Frey, N. (2011). Feedback and Feed Forward. *Principal Leadership.* 11 no9 My2011, p. 90-3. Reston, VA. National Association of Secondary Principals.

Fisher, D., Frey, N, & Hattie, J. (2016). *Visible learning for literacy, grades k-12: Implementing the practices that work best to accelerate student learning.* Thousand Oaks, CA. Corwin.

Fisher, D., Frey, N., J. Hattie, & Thayre, M. (2017). *Teaching literacy in the visible learning classroom, grades 6-12*. Thousand Oaks, CA. Corwin.

Wormeli, R. (2010, November 30) Formative and Summative Assessment. Retrieved from YouTube. Nov 30, 2010.

CPSIA information can be obtained
at www.ICGtesting.com
Printed in the USA
LVHW091500041019
633216LV00001B/189/P